THE BANQUET OF PLATO TRANSLATED FROM THE GREEK BY PERCY BYSSHE SHELLEY

Copyright © 2011 Read Books Ltd.
This book is copyright and may not be
reproduced or copied in any way without
the express permission of the publisher in writing

British Library Cataloguing-in-Publication Data
A catalogue record for this book is available from
the British Library

PERCY BYSSHE SHELLEY

Percy Bysshe Shelley was born in Horsham, Sussex, England in 1792. He studied at University College, Oxford, but his atheistic views got him expelled. Estranged from his father, he left home and began to take trips to London to spend time with famous journalist William Godwin. It was here, around the time that he published *Queen Mab: A Philosophical Poem* (1813), that Shelley met the Godwin's daughter, Mary, quickly striking up a romantic relationship with her. In 1814, the two of them eloped to Switzerland, where they spent time with Lord Byron, and where the young Mary Shelley found the inspiration for her future masterpiece, *Frankenstein* (1818).

In 1815, the Shelleys moved back to London, where the two of them continued to write. Percy was a prolific producer of literature, and many of the verse works he penned in the last seven or eight years of his life – such as *Ozymandias, Ode to the West Wind, To a Skylark, Music, When Soft Voices Die, The Cloud* and *The Masque of Anarchy* – are now considered some of the best in the English language. He was also known for his uncompromising idealism, most notably as a fierce advocate of non-violence and vegetarianism. Shelley spent the latter part of life in Italy, where he drowned during a sailing trip in 1822, aged just 29. It wasn't until after his passing that he developed a large following, and since his death writers as varied as George Bernard Shaw, Bertrand Russell and Karl Marx have all expressed their admiration for him.

THE PERSONS OF THE DIALOGUE

Apollodorus
A Friend of Apollodorus
Glauco
Aristodemus
Socrates
Agathon
Phædrus
Pausanias
Eryximachus
Aristophanes
Diotima
Alcibiades

THE BANQUET OF PLATO

APOLLODORUS. I think that the subject of your inquiries is still fresh in my memory; for yesterday, as I chanced to be returning home from Phaleros, one of my acquaintance, seeing me before him, called out to me from a distance, jokingly, 'Apollodorus, you Phalerian, will you not wait a minute?'—I waited for him, and as soon as he overtook me, 'I have just been looking for you, Apollodorus,' he said, 'for I wish to hear what those discussions were on Love, which took place at the party, when Agathon, Socrates, Alcibiades, and some others met at supper. Some one who heard it from Phœnix, the son of Philip, told me that you could give a full account, but he could relate nothing distinctly himself. Relate to me, then, I entreat you, all the circumstances. I know you are a faithful reporter of the discussions of your friends; but first tell me, were you present at the party or not?'

'Your informant,' I replied, 'seems to have given you no very clear idea of what you wish to hear, if he thinks that these discussions took place so lately as that I could have been of the party.'—'Indeed, I thought so,' replied he.—'For how,' said I, 'O Glauco! could I have been present? Do you not know that Agathon has been absent from the city many years? But, since I began to converse with Socrates, and to observe each day all his words and actions, three years are scarcely past. Before this time I wandered about wherever it might chance, thinking that I did something, but being, in truth, a most miserable wretch, not less than you are now, who believe that you ought to do anything rather than practise the love of wisdom.'—'Do not cavil,' interrupted Glauco, 'but tell me, when did this party take place?'

'Whilst we were yet children,' I replied, 'when Agathon first gained the prize of tragedy, and the day after that on which he and the chorus made sacrifices in celebration of their success.'—'A long time ago, it seems. But who told you all the circumstances of the discussion? Did you hear them from Socrates himself?'—'No, by Jupiter! but the same person from whom Phœnix had his information, one Aristodemus, a Cydathenean,—a little man who always went about without sandals. He was present at this feast, being, I believe, more than any of his contemporaries, a lover and admirer of Socrates. I have questioned Socrates concerning some of the circumstances of his narration, who confirms all that I have heard from Aristodemus.'—'Why, then,' said Glauco, 'why not relate them, as we walk, to me? The road to the city is every way convenient, both for those who listen and those who speak.'

Thus as we walked I gave him some account of those discussions concerning Love; since, as I said before, I remember them with sufficient accuracy. If I am required to relate them also to you, that shall willingly be done; for whensoever either I myself talk of philosophy, or listen to others talking of it, in addition to the improvement which I conceive there arises from such conversation, I am delighted beyond measure; but whenever I hear your discussions about moneyed men and great proprietors, I am weighed down with grief, and pity you, who, doing nothing, believe that you are doing something. Perhaps you think that I am a miserable wretch; and, indeed, I believe that you think truly. I do not think, but well know, that you are miserable.

COMPANION. You are always the same, Apollodorus—always saying some ill of yourself and others. Indeed, you seem to me to think every one miserable except Socrates, beginning with yourself. I do not know what could have entitled you to the surname of the 'Madman,' for I am sure you are consistent enough, forever inveighing with bitterness against yourself and all others except Socrates.

APOLLODORUS. My dear friend, it is manifest that I am out of my wits from this alone—that I have such opinions as you describe concerning myself and you.

COMPANION. It is not worth while, Apollodorus, to dispute now about these things; but do what I entreat you, and relate to us what were these discussions.

APOLLODORUS. They were such as I will proceed to tell you. But let me attempt to relate them in the order which Aristodemus observed in relating them to me. He said that he met Socrates washed, and, contrary to his usual custom, sandalled, and having inquired whither he went so gaily dressed, Socrates replied, 'I am going to sup at Agathon's; yesterday I avoided it, disliking the crowd, which would attend at the prize sacrifices then celebrated; to-day I promised to be there, and I made myself so gay, because one ought to be beautiful to approach one who is beautiful. But you, Aristodemus, what think you of coming uninvited to supper?'—'I will do,' he replied, 'as you command.'—'Follow, then, that we may, by changing its application, disarm that proverb which says, "To the feasts of the good, the good come uninvited." Homer, indeed, seems not only to destroy, but to outrage the proverb; for, describing Agamemnon as excellent in battle, and Menelaus but a faint-hearted warrior, he represents Menelaus as coming uninvited to the feast of one better and braver than himself.'—Aristodemus, hearing this, said, 'I also am in some danger, Socrates, not as you say, but according to Homer, of approaching like an unworthy inferior the banquet of one more wise and excellent than myself. Will you not, then, make some excuse for me? for I shall not confess that I came uninvited, but shall say that I was invited by you.'—'As we walk together,' said Socrates, 'we will consider together what excuse to make —but let us go.'

Thus discoursing, they proceeded. But as they walked, Socrates, engaged in some deep contemplation, slackened his pace, and, observing Aristodemus waiting for him, he desired him to go on before. When Aristodemus arrived at Agathon's house he found the door open, and it occurred, somewhat comically, that a slave met him at the vestibule, and conducted him where he found the guests already reclined. As soon as Agathon saw him, 'You arrive just in time to sup with us, Aristodemus,' he said; 'if you have any other purpose in your visit, defer it to a better opportunity. I was looking for you yesterday, to invite you to be of our party; I could not find you anywhere. But how is it that you do not bring Socrates with you?'

But he, turning round and not seeing Socrates behind him, said to Agathon, 'I just came hither in his company, being invited by him to sup with you.' —'You did well,' replied Agathon, 'to come; but where is Socrates?'— 'He just now came hither behind me; I myself wonder where he can be.'— 'Go and look, boy,' said Agathon, 'and bring Socrates in; meanwhile, you, Aristodemus, recline there near Eryximachus.' And he bade a slave wash his feet that he might recline. Another slave, meanwhile, brought word that Socrates had retired into a neighbouring vestibule, where he stood, and, in spite of his message, refused to come in.—'What absurdity you talk!' cried Agathon; 'call him, and do not leave him till he comes.'—'Let him alone, by all means,' said Aristodemus; 'it is customary with him sometimes to retire in this way and stand wherever it may chance. He will come presently, I do not doubt; do not disturb him.' —'Well, be it as you will,' said Agathon; 'as it is, you boys, bring supper for the rest; put before us what you will, for I resolved that there should be no master of the feast. Consider me and these my friends as guests, whom you have invited to supper, and serve them so that we may commend you.' After this they began supper, but Socrates did not come in. Agathon ordered him to be called, but Aristodemus perpetually forbade it. At last he came in, much about the middle of supper, not having delayed so long as was his custom. Agathon (who happened to be reclining at the end of the table, and alone) said, as he entered, 'Come hither, Socrates, and sit down by me; so that by the mere touch of one so wise as you are, I may enjoy the fruit of your meditations in the vestibule; for I well know, you would not have departed till you had discovered and secured it.' Socrates, having sate down as he was desired, replied, 'It would be well, Agathon, if wisdom were of such a nature, as that when we touched each other, it would overflow of its own accord, from him who possesses much to him who possesses little; like the water in two chalices, which will flow through a flock of wool from the fuller into the emptier, until both are equal. If wisdom had this property, I should esteem myself most fortunate in reclining near to you. I should thus soon be filled, I think, with the most beautiful and various wisdom. Mine, indeed, is something obscure, and doubtful, and dreamlike. But yours is radiant, and has been crowned with amplest reward; for though you are yet so young, it shone forth from you, and became so manifest yesterday, that more than thirty thousand Greeks can bear testimony to its excellence and loveliness.'—'You are laughing at me, Socrates,' said Agathon; 'but you and I will decide this controversy about wisdom by and by, taking Bacchus for our judge. At present turn to your supper.'

After Socrates and the rest had finished supper, and had reclined back on their couches, and the libations had been poured forth, and they had sung hymns to the god, and all other rites which are customary had been performed, they turned to drinking. Then Pausanias made this kind of proposal. 'Come, my friends,' said he, 'in what manner will it be pleasantest for us to drink? I must confess to you that, in reality, I am not very well from the wine we drank last night, and I have need of some intermission. I suspect that most of you are in the same condition, for you were here yesterday. Now consider how we shall drink most easily and comfortably.'

"'Tis a good proposal, Pausanias,' said Aristophanes, 'to contrive, in some way or other, to place moderation in our cups. I was one of those who were drenched last night.'—Eryximachus, the son of Acumenius, hearing this, said, 'I am of your opinion; I only wish to know one thing—whether Agathon is in the humour for hard drinking?'—'Not at all,' replied Agathon; 'I confess that I am not able to drink much this evening.'—'It is an excellent thing for us,' replied Eryximachus—'I mean myself, Aristodemus, Phædrus, and these others—if you, who are such invincible drinkers, now refuse to drink. I ought to except Socrates, for he is capable of drinking everything or nothing; and whatever we shall determine will equally suit him. Since, then, no one present has

any desire to drink much wine, I shall perhaps give less offence if I declare the nature of drunkenness. The science of medicine teaches us that drunkenness is very pernicious; nor would I choose to drink immoderately myself, or counsel another to do so, especially if he had been drunk the night before.'
—'Yes,' said Phædrus, the Myrinusian, interrupting him, 'I have been accustomed to confide in you, especially in your directions concerning medicine; and I would now willingly do so, if the rest will do the same.' All then agreed that they would drink at this present banquet not for drunkenness, but for pleasure.

'Since, then,' said Eryximachus, 'it is decided that no one shall be compelled to drink more than he pleases, I think that we may as well send away the flute-player to play to herself; or, if she likes, to the women within. Let us devote the present occasion to conversation between ourselves, and if you wish, I will propose to you what shall be the subject of our discussion.' All present desired and entreated that he would explain. 'The exordium of my speech,' said Eryximachus, 'will be in the style of the Menalippe of Euripides, for the story which I am about to tell belongs not to me, but to Phædrus. Phædrus has often indignantly complained to me, saying, "Is it not strange, Eryximachus, that there are innumerable hymns and pæans composed for the other gods, but that not one of the many poets who spring up in the world has ever composed a verse in honour of Love, who is such and so great a god? Nor any one of those accomplished sophists, who, like the famous Prodicus, have celebrated the praise of Hercules and others, has ever celebrated that of Love; but, what is more astonishing, I have lately met with the book of some philosopher, in which salt is extolled on account of its utility, and many other things of the same nature are in like manner extolled with elaborate praise. That so much serious thought is expended on such trifles, and that no man has dared to this day to frame a hymn in honour of Love, who being so great a deity is thus neglected, may well be sufficient to excite my indignation."

'There seemed to me some justice in these complaints of Phædrus; I propose, therefore, at the same time for the sake of giving pleasure to Phædrus, and that we may on the present occasion do something well and befitting us, that this god should receive from those who are now present the honour which is most due to him. If you agree to my proposal, an excellent discussion might arise on the subject. Every one ought, according to my plan, to praise Love with as much eloquence as he can. Let Phædrus begin first, both because he reclines the first in order, and because he is the father of the discussion.'

'No one will vote against you, Eryximachus,' said Socrates, 'for how can I oppose your proposal, who am ready to confess that I know nothing on any subject but love? Or how can Agathon, or Pausanias, or even Aristophanes, whose life is one perpetual ministration to Venus and Bacchus? Or how can any other whom I see here? Though we who sit last are scarcely on an equality with you; for if those who speak before us shall have exhausted the subject with their eloquence and reasonings, our discourses will be superfluous. But in the name of Good Fortune, let Phædrus begin and praise Love.' The whole party agreed to what Socrates said, and entreated Phædrus to begin.

What each then said on this subject, Aristodemus did not entirely recollect, nor do I recollect all that he related to me; but only the speeches of those who said what was most worthy of remembrance. First, then, Phædrus began thus:—

'Love is a mighty deity, and the object of admiration, both to gods and men, for many and for various claims; but especially on account of his origin. For that he is to be honoured as one of the most ancient of the gods, this may serve as a testimony—that Love has no parents, nor is there any poet or other person who has ever affirmed that there are such. Hesiod says, that first "Chaos was produced; then the broad-bosomed Earth, to be a secure foundation for all things; then Love." He says, that after Chaos these two were produced, the Earth and Love. Parmenides, speaking of generation, says:—"But he created Love before any of the gods." Acusileus agrees with Hesiod. Love, therefore, is universally acknowledged to be among the oldest of things. And in addition to this, Love is the author of our greatest advantages; for I cannot imagine a greater happiness and advantage to one who is in the flower of youth than an amiable lover, or to a lover than an amiable object of his love. For neither birth, nor wealth, nor honours, can awaken in the minds of men the principles which should guide those who from their youth aspire to an honourable and excellent life, as Love awakens them. I speak of the fear of shame, which deters them from that which is disgraceful; and the love of glory, which incites to honourable deeds. For it is not possible that a state or private person should accomplish, without these incitements, anything beautiful or great. I assert, then, that should one who loves be discovered in any dishonourable action, or tamely enduring insult through cowardice, he would feel more anguish and shame if observed by the object of his passion than if he were observed by his father, or his companions, or any other person. In like manner, among warmly attached friends, a man is especially grieved to be discovered by his friend in any dishonourable act. If then, by any contrivance, a state or army could be composed of friends bound by strong attachment, it is beyond calculation how excellently they would administer their affairs, refraining from anything base, contending with each other for the acquirement of fame, and exhibiting such valour in battle as that, though few in numbers, they might subdue all mankind. For should one friend desert the ranks or cast away his arms in the presence of the other, he would suffer far acuter shame from that one person's regard, than from the regard of all other men. A thousand times would he prefer to die, rather than desert the object of his attachment, and not succour him in danger.

'There is none so worthless whom Love cannot impel, as it were by a divine inspiration, towards virtue, even so that he may through this inspiration become equal to one who might naturally be more excellent; and, in truth, as Homer says, the God breathes vigour into certain heroes—so Love breathes into those who love, the spirit which is produced from himself. Not only men, but even women who love, are those alone who willingly expose themselves to die for others. Alcestis, the daughter of Pelias, affords to the Greeks a remarkable example of this opinion; she alone being willing to die for her husband, and so surpassing his parents in the affection with which love inspired her towards him, as to make them appear, in the comparison with her, strangers to their own child, and related to him merely in name; and so lovely and admirable did this action appear, not only to men, but even to the Gods, that, although they conceded the prerogative of bringing back the spirit from death to few among the many who then performed excellent and honourable deeds, yet, delighted with this action, they redeemed her soul from the infernal regions: so highly do the Gods honour zeal and devotion in love. They sent back indeed Orpheus, the son of Œagrus, from Hell, with his purpose unfulfilled, and, showing him only the spectre of her for whom he came, refused to render up herself. For Orpheus seemed to them, not, as Alcestis, to have dared die for the sake of her whom he loved, and thus to secure to himself a perpetual intercourse with her in the regions to which she had preceded him, but, like a cowardly musician, to have contrived to descend alive into Hell; and, indeed, they appointed as a punishment for his cowardice that he should be put to death by women.

'Far otherwise did they reward Achilles, the son of Thetis, whom they sent to inhabit the islands of the blessed. For Achilles, though informed by his mother that his own death would ensue upon his killing Hector, but that if he refrained from it he might return home and die in old age, yet preferred revenging and honouring his beloved Patroclus; not to die for him merely, but to disdain and reject that life which he had ceased to share. Therefore the Greeks honoured Achilles beyond all other men, because he thus preferred his friend to all things else. 'On this account have the Gods rewarded Achilles more amply than Alcestis; permitting his spirit to inhabit the islands of the blessed. Hence do I assert that Love is the most ancient and venerable of deities, and most powerful to endow mortals with the possession of happiness and virtue, both whilst they live and after they die.'

Thus Aristodemus reported the discourse of Phædrus; and after Phædrus, he said that some others spoke, whose discourses he did not well remember. When they had ceased, Pausanias began thus:—

'Simply to praise Love, O Phædrus, seems to me too bounded a scope for our discourse. If Love were one, it would be well. But since Love is not one, I will endeavour to distinguish which is the Love whom it becomes us to praise, and, having thus discriminated one from the other, will attempt to render him who is the subject of our discourse the honour due to his divinity. We all know that Venus is never without Love; and if Venus were one, Love would be one; but since there are two Venuses, of necessity also must there be two Loves. For assuredly are there two Venuses; one, the eldest, the daughter of Uranus, born without a mother, whom we call the Uranian; the other younger, the daughter of Jupiter and Dione, whom we call the Pandemian;—of necessity must there also be two Loves, the Uranian and Pandemian companions of these goddesses. It is becoming to praise all the Gods, but the attributes which fall to the lot of each may be distinguished and selected. For any particular action whatever, in itself is neither good nor evil; what we are now doing —drinking, singing, talking, none of these things are good in themselves, but the mode in which they are done stamps them with its own nature; and that which is done well is good, and that which is done ill is evil. Thus, not all love, nor every mode of love is beautiful, or worthy of commendation, but that alone which excites us to love worthily. The Love, therefore, which attends upon Venus Pandemos is, in truth, common to the vulgar, and presides over transient and fortuitous connections, and is worshipped by the least excellent of mankind. The votaries of this deity seek the body rather than the soul, and the ignorant rather than the wise, disdaining all that is honourable and lovely, and considering how they shall best satisfy their sensual necessities. This love is derived from the younger goddess, who partakes in her nature both of male and female. But the attendant on the other, the Uranian, whose nature is entirely masculine, is the Love who inspires us with affection, and exempts us from all wantonness and libertinism. Those who are inspired by this divinity seek the affections of those who are endowed by nature with greater excellence and vigour both of body and mind. And it is easy to distinguish those who especially exist under the influence of this power, by their choosing in early youth as the objects of their love those in whom the intellectual faculties have begun to develop. For those who begin to love in this manner seem to me to be preparing to pass their whole life together in a community of good and evil, and not ever lightly deceiving those who love them, to be faithless to their vows. There ought to be a law that none should love the very young: so much serious affection as this deity enkindles should not be doubtfully bestowed; for the body and mind of those so young are yet unformed, and it is difficult to foretell what will be their future tendencies and power. The good voluntarily impose this law upon themselves, and those vulgar lovers ought to be compelled to the same observance, as we deter them with all the power of the laws from the love of free matrons. For these are the persons whose shameful actions embolden those who observe their importunity and intemperance, to assert that it is dishonourable to serve and gratify the objects of our love. But no one who does this gracefully, and according to law, can justly be liable to the imputation of blame.

'Not only friendship, but philosophy and the practice of the gymnastic exercises, are represented as dishonourable by the tyrannical governments under which the barbarians live. For I imagine it would little conduce to the benefit of the governors, that the governed should be disciplined to lofty thoughts and to the unity and communion of steadfast friendship, of which admirable effects the tyrants of our own country have also learned that Love is the author. For the love of Harmodius and Aristogeiton, strengthened into a firm friendship, dissolved the tyranny. Wherever, therefore, it is declared dishonourable in any case to serve and benefit friends, that law is a mark of the depravity of the legislator, the avarice and tyranny of the rulers, and the cowardice of those who are ruled. Wherever it is simply declared to be honourable without distinction of cases, such a declaration denotes dulness and want of subtlety of mind in the authors of the regulation. Here the degrees of praise or blame to be attributed by law are far better regulated; but it is yet difficult to determine the cases to which they should refer.

'It is evident, however, for one in whom passion is enkindled, it is more honourable to love openly than secretly; and most honourable to love the most excellent and virtuous, even if they should be less beautiful than others. It is honourable for the lover to exhort and sustain the object of his love in virtuous conduct. It is considered honourable to attain the love of those whom we seek, and the contrary shameful; and to facilitate this attainment, opinion has given to the lover the permission of acquiring favour by the most extraordinary devices, which if a person should practise for any purpose besides this, he would incur the severest reproof of philosophy. For if any one desirous of accumulating money, or ambitious of procuring power, or seeking any other advantage, should, like a lover seeking to acquire the favour of his beloved, employ prayers and entreaties in his necessity, and swear such oaths as lovers swear, and sleep before the threshold, and offer to subject himself to such slavery as no slave even would endure, he would be frustrated of the attainment of what he sought, both by his enemies and friends; these reviling him for his flattery, those sharply admonishing him, and taking to themselves the shame of his servility. But there is a certain grace in a lover who does all these things, so that he alone may do them without dishonour. It is commonly said that the Gods accord pardon to the lover alone if he should break his oath, and that there is no oath by Venus. Thus, as our law declares, both Gods and men have given to lovers all possible indulgence. 'The affair, however, I imagine, stands thus: As I have before said, love cannot be considered in itself as either honourable or dishonourable: if it is honourably pursued, it is honourable; if dishonourably, dishonourable; it is dishonourable basely to serve and gratify a worthless person; it is honourable honourably to serve a person of virtue. That Pandemic lover who loves rather the body than the soul is worthless, nor can be constant and consistent, since he has placed his affections on that which has no stability. For as soon as the flower of the form, which was the sole object of his desire, has faded, then he departs and is seen no more; bound by no faith nor shame of his many promises and persuasions. But he who is the lover of virtuous manners is constant during life, since he has placed himself in harmony and desire with that which is consistent with itself.

'These two classes of persons we ought to distinguish with careful examination, so that we may serve and converse with the one and avoid the other; determining, by that inquiry, by what a man is attracted, and for what the object of his love is dear to him. On the same account it is considered as dishonourable to be inspired with love at once, lest time should be wanting to know and approve the character of the object. It is considered dishonourable to be captivated by the allurements of wealth and power, or terrified through injuries to yield up the affections, or not to despise in the comparison with an unconstrained choice all political influence and personal advantage. For no circumstance is there in wealth or power so invariable and consistent, as that no generous friendship can ever spring up from amongst them. We have an opinion with respect to lovers which declares that it shall not be considered servile or disgraceful, though the lover should submit himself to any species of slavery for the sake of his beloved. The same opinion holds with respect to those who undergo any degradation for the sake of virtue. And also it is esteemed among us, that if any one chooses to serve and obey another for the purpose of becoming more wise or more virtuous through the intercourse that might thence arise, such willing slavery is not the slavery of a dishonest flatterer. Through this we should consider in the same light a servitude undertaken for the sake of love as one undertaken for the acquirement of wisdom or any other excellence, if indeed the devotion of a lover to his beloved is to be considered a beautiful thing. For when the lover and the beloved have once arrived at the same point, the province of each being distinguished: the one able to assist in the cultivation of the mind and in the acquirement of every other excellence; the other yet requiring education, and seeking the possession of wisdom; then alone, by the union of these conditions, and in no other case, is it honourable for the beloved to yield up the affections to the lover. In this servitude alone there is no disgrace in being deceived and defeated of the object for which it was undertaken; whereas every other is disgraceful, whether we are deceived or no.

'On the same principle, if any one seeks the friendship of another, believing him to be virtuous, for the sake of becoming better through such intercourse and affection, and is deceived, his friend turning out to be worthless, and far from the possession of virtue; yet it is honourable to have been so deceived. For such a one seems to have submitted to a kind of servitude, because he would endure anything for the sake of becoming more virtuous and wise; a disposition of mind eminently beautiful.

'This is that Love who attends on the Uranian deity, and is Uranian; the author of innumerable benefits both to the state and to individuals, and by the necessity of whose influence those who love are disciplined into the zeal of virtue. All other loves are the attendants on Venus Pandemos. So much, although unpremeditated, is what I have to deliver on the subject of Love, O Phædrus.'

Pausanias having ceased (for so the learned teach me to denote the changes of the discourse), Aristodemus said that it came to the turn of Aristophanes to speak; but it happened that, from repletion or some other cause, he had an hiccough which prevented him; so he turned to Eryximachus, the physician, who was reclining close beside him, and said, 'Eryximachus, it is but fair that you should cure my hiccough, or speak instead of me until it is over.'—'I will do both,' said Eryximachus; 'I will speak in your turn, and you, when your hiccough has ceased, shall speak in mine. Meanwhile, if you hold your breath some time, it will subside. If not, gargle your throat with water; and if it still continue, take something to stimulate your nostrils, and sneeze; do this once or twice, and even though it should be very violent, it will cease.'—'Whilst you speak,' said Aristophanes, 'I will follow your directions.'—Eryximachus then began:—

'Since Pausanias, beginning his discourse excellently, placed no fit completion and development to it, I think it necessary to attempt to fill up what he has left unfinished. He has reasoned well in defining Love as of a double nature. The science of medicine, to which I have addicted myself, seems to teach me that the Love which impels towards those who are beautiful, does not subsist only in the souls of men, but in the bodies also of those of all other living beings which are produced upon earth, and, in a word, in all things which are. So wonderful and mighty is this divinity, and so widely is his influence extended over all divine and human things! For the honour of my profession, I will begin by adducing a proof from medicine. The nature of the body contains within itself this double Love. For that which is healthy and that which is diseased in a body differ and are unlike: that which is unlike, loves and desires that which is unlike. Love, therefore, is different in a sane and in a diseased body. Pausanias has asserted rightly that it is honourable to gratify those things in the body which are good and healthy, and in this consists the skill of the physician; whilst those which are bad and diseased ought to be treated with no indulgence. The science of medicine, in a word, is a knowledge of the love affairs of the body, as they bear relation to repletion and evacuation; and he is the most skilful physician who can trace those operations of the good and evil Love, can make the one change places with the other, and attract Love into those parts from which he is absent, or expel him from those which he ought not to occupy. He ought to make those things which are most inimical, friendly, and excite them to mutual love. But those things are most inimical, which are most opposite to each other; cold to heat, bitterness to sweetness, dryness to moisture. Our progenitor, Æsculapius, as the poets inform us (and indeed I believe them), through the skill which he possessed to inspire love and concord in these contending principles, established the science of medicine.

'The gymnastic arts and agriculture, no less than medicine, are exercised under the dominion of this God. Music, as any one may perceive who yields a very slight attention to the subject, originates from the same source; which Heraclitus probably meant, though he could not express his meaning very clearly in words, when he says, "One though apparently differing, yet so agrees with itself, as the harmony of a lyre and a bow." It is great absurdity to say that a harmony differs, and can exist between things whilst they are dissimilar; but probably he meant that from sounds which first differed, like the grave and the acute, and which afterwards agreed, harmony was produced according to musical art. For no harmony can arise from the grave and the acute whilst yet they differ. But harmony is symphony: symphony is, as it were, concord. But it is impossible that concord should subsist between things that differ, so long as they differ. Between things which are discordant and dissimilar there is then no harmony. A rhythm is produced from that which is quick, and that which is slow, first being distinguished and opposed to each other, and then made accordant; so does medicine, no less than music, establish a concord between the objects of its art, producing love and agreement between adverse things.

'Music is, then, the knowledge of that which relates to love in harmony and system. In the very system of harmony and rhythm, it is easy to distinguish love. The double love is not distinguishable in music itself; but it is required to apply it to the service of mankind by system and harmony, which is called poetry, or the composition of melody; or by the correct use of songs and measures already composed, which is called discipline; then one can be distinguished from the other, by the aid of an extremely skilful artist. And the better love ought to be honoured and preserved for the sake of those who are virtuous, and that the nature of the vicious may be changed through the inspiration of its spirit. This is that beautiful Uranian Love, the attendant on the Uranian muse: the Pandemian is the attendant of Polyhymnia; to whose influence we should only so far subject ourselves as to derive pleasure from it without indulging to excess; in the same manner as, according to our art, we are instructed to seek the pleasures of the table only so far as we can enjoy them without the consequences of disease. In music, therefore, and in medicine, and in all other things, human and divine, this double love ought to be traced and discriminated, for it is in all things.

'Even the constitution of the seasons of the year is penetrated with these contending principles. For so often as heat and cold, dryness and moisture, of which I spoke before, are influenced by the more benignant love, and are harmoniously and temperately intermingled with the seasons, they bring maturity and health to men, and to all the other animals and plants. But when the evil and injurious love assumes the dominion of the seasons of the year, destruction is spread widely abroad. Then pestilence is accustomed to arise, and many other blights and diseases fall upon animals and plants:

and hoar frosts, and hails, and mildew on the corn are produced from that excessive and disorderly love with which each season of the year is impelled towards the other; the motions of which, and the knowledge of the stars, is called astronomy. All sacrifices, and all those things in which divination is concerned (for these things are the links by which is maintained an intercourse and communion between the Gods and men), are nothing else than the science of preservation and right government of love. For impiety is accustomed to spring up so soon as any one ceases to serve the more honourable love, and worship him by the sacrifice of good actions; but submits himself to the influences of the other, in relation to his duties towards his parents and the Gods, and the living and the dead. It is the object of divination to distinguish and remedy the effects of these opposite loves; and divination is therefore the author of the friendship of Gods and men, because it affords the knowledge of what in matters of love is lawful or unlawful to men.

'Thus every species of love possesses collectively a various and vast, or rather universal power. But love which incites to the acquirement of its objects according to virtue and wisdom, possesses the most exclusive dominion, and prepares for his worshippers the highest happiness through the mutual intercourse of social kindness which it promotes among them, and through the benevolence which he attracts to them from the Gods, our superiors.

'Probably in thus praising love, I have unwillingly omitted many things; but it is your business, O Aristophanes, to fill up all that I have left incomplete; or if you have imagined any other mode of honouring the divinity; for I observe your hiccough is over.'

'Yes,' said Aristophanes, 'but not before I applied the sneezing. I wonder why the harmonious construction of our body should require such noisy operations as sneezing; for it ceased the moment I sneezed.'—'Do you not observe what you do, my good Aristophanes?' said Eryximachus; 'you are going to speak, and you predispose us to laughter, and compel me to watch for the first ridiculous idea which you may start in your discourse, when you might have spoken in peace.'—'Let me unsay what I have said, then,' replied Aristophanes, laughing. 'Do not watch me, I entreat you; though I am

not afraid of saying what is laughable (since that would be all gain, and quite in the accustomed spirit of my muse), but lest I should say what is ridiculous.'
—'Do you think to throw your dart, and escape with impunity, Aristophanes? Attend, and what you say be careful you maintain; then, perhaps, if it pleases me, I may dismiss you without question.'

'Indeed, Eryximachus,' proceeded Aristophanes, 'I have designed that my discourse should be very different from yours and that of Pausanias. It seems to me that mankind are by no means penetrated with a conception of the power of Love, or they would have built sumptuous temples and altars, and have established magnificent rites of sacrifice in his honour; he deserves worship and homage more than all the other Gods, and he has yet received none. For Love is of all the Gods the most friendly to mortals, and the physician of those wounds whose cure would be the greatest happiness which could be conferred upon the human race. I will endeavour to unfold to you his true power, and you can relate what I declare to others.

'You ought first to know the nature of man, and the adventures he has gone through; for his nature was anciently far different from that which it is at present. First, then, human beings were formerly not divided into two sexes, male and female; there was also a third, common to both the others, the name of which remains, though the sex itself has disappeared. The androgynous sex, both in appearance and in name, was common both to male and female; its name alone remains, which labours under a reproach.

'At the period to which I refer, the form of every human being was round, the back and the sides being circularly joined, and each had four arms and as many legs; two faces fixed upon a round neck, exactly like each other; one head between the two faces; four ears, and everything else as from such proportions it is easy to conjecture. Man walked upright as now, in whatever direction he pleased; but when he wished to go fast he made use of all his eight limbs, and proceeded in a rapid motion by rolling circularly round—like tumblers, who with their legs in the air tumble round and round. We account for the production of three sexes by supposing that, at the beginning, the male was produced from the sun, the female from the earth; and that sex which participated in both sexes, from the moon, by reason of the androgynous nature of the moon. They were round, and their mode of proceeding was round, from the similarity which must needs subsist between them and their parent.

'They were strong also, and had aspiring thoughts. They it was who levied war against the Gods; and what Homer writes concerning Ephialtus and Otus, that they sought to ascend heaven and dethrone the Gods, in reality relates to this primitive people. Jupiter and the other Gods debated what was to be done in this emergency. For neither could they prevail on themselves to destroy them, as they had the giants, with thunder, so that the race should be abolished; for in that case they would be deprived of the honours of the sacrifices which they were in the custom of receiving from them; nor could they permit a continuance of their insolence and impiety. Jupiter, with some difficulty having desired silence, at length spoke. "I think," said he, "I have contrived a method by which we may, by rendering the human race more feeble, quell the insolence which they exercise, without proceeding to their utter destruction. I will cut each of them in half; and so they will at once be weaker and more useful on account of their numbers. They shall walk upright on two legs. If they show any more insolence, and will not keep quiet, I will cut them up in half again, so they shall go about hopping on one leg."

'So saying, he cut human beings in

half, as people cut eggs before they salt them, or as I have seen eggs cut with hairs. He ordered Apollo to take each one as he cut him, and turn his face and half his neck towards the operation, so that by contemplating it he might become more cautious and humble; and then, to cure him, Apollo turned the face round, and drawing the skin upon what we now call the belly, like a contracted pouch, and leaving one opening, that which is called the navel, tied it in the middle. He then smoothed many other wrinkles, and moulded the breast with much such an instrument as the leather-cutters use to smooth the skins upon the block. He left only a few wrinkles in the belly, near the navel, to serve as a record of its former adventure. Immediately after this division, as each desired to possess the other half of himself, these divided people threw their arms around and embraced each other, seeking to grow together; and from this resolution to do nothing without the other half, they died of hunger and weakness: when one half died and the other was left alive, that which was thus left sought the other and folded it to its bosom; whether that half were an entire woman (for we now call it a woman) or a man; and thus they perished. But Jupiter, pitying them, thought of another contrivance.... In this manner is generation now produced, by the union of male and female; so that from the embrace of a man and woman the race is propagated.

'From this period, mutual love has naturally existed between human beings; that reconciler and bond of union of their original nature, which seeks to make two one, and to heal the divided nature of man. Every one of us is thus the half of what may be properly termed a man, and like a psetta cut in two, is the imperfect portion of an entire whole, perpetually necessitated to seek the half belonging to him. 'Such as I have described is ever an affectionate lover and a faithful friend, delighting in that which is in conformity with his own nature. Whenever, therefore, any such as I have described are impetuously struck, through the sentiment of their former union, with love and desire and the want of community, they are unwilling to be divided even for a moment. These are they who devote their whole lives to each other, with a vain and inexpressible longing to obtain from each other something they know not what; for it is not merely the sensual delights of their intercourse for the sake of which they dedicate themselves to each other with such serious affection; but the soul of each manifestly thirsts for, from the other, something which there are no words to describe, and divines that which it seeks, and traces obscurely the footsteps of its obscure desire. If Vulcan should say to persons thus affected, "My good people, what is it that you want with one another?" And if, while they were hesitating what to answer, he should proceed to ask, "Do you not desire the closest union and singleness to exist between you, so that you may never be divided night or day? If so, I will melt you together, and make you grow into one, so that both in life and death ye may be undivided. Consider, is this what you desire? Will it content you if you become that which I propose?" we all know that no one would refuse such an offer, but would at once feel that this was what he had ever sought; and intimately to mix and melt and to be melted together with his beloved, so that one should be made out of two.

'The cause of this desire is, that according to our original nature, we were once entire. The desire and the pursuit of integrity and union is that which we all love. First, as I said, we were entire, but now we have been dwindled through our own weakness, as the Arcadians by the Lacedæmonians. There is reason to fear, if we are guilty of any additional impiety towards the Gods, that we may be cut in two again, and may go about like those figures painted on the columns, divided through the middle of our nostrils, as thin as lispæ. On which account every man ought to be exhorted to pay due reverence to the Gods, that we may escape so severe a punishment, and obtain those things which Love, our general and commander, incites us to desire; against whom let none rebel by exciting the hatred of the Gods. For if we continue on good terms with them, we may discover and possess those lost and concealed objects of our love, a good-fortune which now befalls to few.

'I assert, then, that the happiness of all, both men and women, consists singly in the fulfilment of their love, and in that possession of its objects by which we are in some degree restored to our ancient nature. If this be the completion of felicity, that must necessarily approach nearest to it in which we obtain the possession and society of those whose natures most intimately accord with our own. And if we would celebrate any God as the author of this benefit, we should justly celebrate Love with hymns of joy; who, in our present condition, brings good assistance in our necessity, and affords great hopes, if we persevere in piety towards the Gods, that he will restore us to our original state, and confer on us the complete happiness alone suited to our nature.

'Such, Eryximachus, is my discourse on the subject of Love; different indeed from yours, which I nevertheless entreat you not to turn into ridicule, that we may not interrupt what each has separately to deliver on the subject.'

'I will refrain at present,' said Eryximachus, 'for your discourse delighted me. And if I did not know that Socrates and Agathon were profoundly versed in the science of love affairs, I should fear that they had nothing new to say, after so many and such various imaginations. As it is, I confide in the fertility of their geniuses.'—'Your part of the contest at least was strenuously fought, Eryximachus,' said Socrates, 'but if you had been in the situation in which I am, or rather shall be, after the discourse of Agathon, like me you would then have reason to fear, and be reduced to your wits' end.'—'Socrates,' said Agathon, 'wishes to confuse me with the enchantments of his wit, sufficiently confused already with the expectation I see in the assembly in favour of my discourse.'—'I must have lost my memory, Agathon,' replied Socrates, 'if I imagined that you could be disturbed by a few private persons, after having witnessed your firmness and courage in ascending the rostrum with the actors, and in calmly reciting your compositions in the presence of so great an assembly as that which decreed you the prize of tragedy.'—'What, then, Socrates,' retorted Agathon, 'do you think me so full of the theatre as to be ignorant that the judgment of a few wise is more awful than that of a multitude of others, to one who rightly balances the value of their suffrages?'— 'I should judge ill indeed, Agathon,' answered Socrates, 'in thinking you capable of any rude and unrefined conception, for I well know that if you meet with any whom you consider wise, you esteem such alone of more value than all others. But we are far from being entitled to this distinction, for we were also of that assembly, and to be numbered among the rest. But should you meet with any who are really wise, you would be careful to say nothing in their presence which you thought they would not approve—is it not so?'—'Certainly,' replied Agathon.—'You would not then exercise the same caution in the presence of the multitude in which they were included?'—'My dear Agathon,' said Phædrus, interrupting him, 'if you answer all the questions of Socrates, they will never have an end; he will urge them without conscience so long as he can get any person, especially one who is so beautiful, to dispute with him. I own it delights me to hear Socrates discuss; but at present I must see that Love is not defrauded of the praise, which it is my province to exact from each of you. Pay the God his due, and then reason between yourselves if you will.'

'Your admonition is just, Phædrus,' replied Agathon, 'nor need any reasoning I hold with Socrates impede me: we shall find many future opportunities for discussion. I will begin my discourse, then, first having defined what ought to be the subject of it. All who have already spoken seem to me not so much to have praised Love, as to have felicitated mankind on the many advantages of which that deity is the cause; what he is, the author of these great benefits, none have yet declared. There is one mode alone of celebration which would comprehend the whole topic, namely, first to declare what are those benefits, and then what he is who is the author of those benefits, which are the subject of our discourse. Love ought first to be praised, and then his gifts declared. I assert, then, that although all the Gods are immortally happy, Love, if I dare trust my voice to express so awful a truth, is the happiest, and most excellent, and the most beautiful. That he is the most beautiful is evident; first, O Phædrus, from this circumstance, that he is the youngest of the Gods; and secondly, from his fleetness, and from his repugnance to all that is old; for he escapes with the swiftness of wings from old age, a thing in itself sufficiently swift, since it overtakes us sooner than there is need; and which Love, who delights in the intercourse of the young, hates, and in no manner can be induced to enter into community with. The ancient proverb, which says that like is attracted by like, applies to the attributes of Love. I concede many things to you, O Phædrus, but this I do not concede, that Love is more ancient than Saturn and Jupiter. I assert that he is not only the youngest of the Gods, but invested with everlasting youth. Those ancient deeds among the Gods recorded by Hesiod and Parmenides, if their relations are to be considered as true, were produced not by Love, but by Necessity. For if Love had been then in Heaven, those violent and sanguinary crimes never would have taken place; but there would ever have subsisted that affection and peace, in which the Gods now live, under the influence of Love.

'He is young, therefore, and being young is tender and soft. There were need of some poet like Homer to celebrate the delicacy and tenderness of Love. For Homer says, that the goddess

Calamity is delicate, and that her feet are tender. "Her feet are soft," he says, "for she treads not upon the ground, but makes her path upon the heads of men." He gives as an evidence of her tenderness, that she walks not upon that which is hard, but that which is soft. The same evidence is sufficient to make manifest the tenderness of Love. For Love walks not upon the earth, nor over the heads of men, which are not indeed very soft; but he dwells within, and treads on the softest of existing things, having established his habitation within the souls and inmost nature of Gods and men; not indeed in all souls—for wherever he chances to find a hard and rugged disposition, there he will not inhabit, but only where it is most soft and tender. Of needs must he be the most delicate of all things, who touches lightly with his feet only the softest parts of those things which are the softest of all.

'He is then the youngest and most delicate of all divinities; and in addition to this he is, as it were, the most moist and liquid. For if he were otherwise he could not, as he does, fold himself around everything, and secretly flow out and into every soul. His loveliness, that which Love possesses far beyond all other things, is a manifestation of the liquid and flowing symmetry of his form; for between deformity and Love there is eternal contrast and repugnance. His life is spent among flowers, and this accounts for the immortal fairness of his skin; for the winged Love rests not in his flight on any form, or within any soul the flower of whose loveliness is faded, but there remains most willingly where is the odour and radiance of blossoms yet unwithered. Concerning the beauty of the God, let this be sufficient, though many things must remain unsaid. Let us next consider the virtue and power of Love.

'What is most admirable in Love is, that he neither inflicts nor endures injury in his relations either with Gods or men. Nor if he suffers anything does he suffer it through violence, nor doing anything does he act it with violence, for Love is never even touched with violence. Every one willingly administers everything to Love; and that which every one voluntarily concedes to another, the laws, which are the kings of the republic, decree that it is just for him to possess. In addition to justice, Love participates in the highest temperance; for if temperance is defined to be the being superior to and holding under dominion pleasures and desires, then Love, than whom no pleasure is more powerful, and who is thus more powerful than all persuasions and delights, must be excellently temperate. In power and valour Mars cannot contend with Love; the love of Venus possesses Mars; the possessor is always superior to the possessed, and he who subdues the most powerful must of necessity be the most powerful of all.

'The justice and temperance and valour of the God have been thus declared; there remains to exhibit his wisdom. And first, that, like Eryximachus, I may honour my own profession, the God is a wise poet; so wise that he can even make a poet one who was not before: for every one, even if before he were ever so undisciplined, becomes a poet as soon as he is touched by Love,—a sufficient proof that Love is a great poet, and well skilled in that science according to the discipline of music. For what any one possesses not, or knows not, that can he neither give nor teach another. And who will deny that the divine poetry, by which all living things are produced upon the earth, is harmonized by the wisdom of Love? Is it not evident that Love was the author of all the arts of life with which we are acquainted, and that he whose teacher has been Love becomes eminent and illustrious, whilst he who knows not Love remains for ever unregarded and obscure? Apollo invented medicine, and divination, and archery, under the guidance of desire and Love; so that Apollo was the disciple of Love. Through him the Muses discovered the arts of literature, and Vulcan that of moulding brass, and Minerva the loom, and Jupiter the mystery of the dominion which he now exercises over Gods and men. So were the Gods taught and disciplined by the love of that which is beautiful, for there is no love towards deformity.

'At the origin of things, as I have before said, many fearful deeds are reported to have been done among the Gods, on account of the dominion of Necessity. But so soon as this deity sprang forth from the desire which for ever tends in the universe towards that which is lovely, then all blessings descended upon all living things, human and divine. Love seems to me, O Phædrus, a divinity the most beautiful and the best of all, and the author to all others of the excellencies with which his own nature is endowed. Nor can I restrain the poetic enthusiasm which takes possession of my discourse, and bids me declare that Love is the divinity who creates peace among men, and calm upon the sea, the windless silence of storms, repose and sleep in sadness. Love divests us of all alienation from each other, and fills our vacant hearts with overflowing sympathy; he gathers us together in such social meetings as we now delight to celebrate, our guardian and our guide in dances, and sacrifices, and feasts. Yes, Love, who showers benignity upon the world, and before whose presence all harsh passions flee and perish; the author of all soft affections; the destroyer of all ungentle thoughts; merciful, mild; the object of the admiration of the wise, and the delight of Gods; possessed by the fortunate, and desired by the unhappy, therefore unhappy because they possess him not; the father of grace, and delicacy, and gentleness, and delight, and persuasion, and desire; the cherisher of all that is good, the abolisher of all evil; our most excellent pilot, defence, saviour, and guardian in labour and in fear, in desire and in reason; the ornament and governor of all things human and divine; the best, the loveliest; in whose footsteps every one ought to follow, celebrating him excellently in song, and bearing each his part in that divinest harmony which Love sings to all things which live and are, soothing the troubled minds of Gods and men. This, O Phædrus, is what I have to offer in praise of the divinity; partly composed, indeed, of thoughtless and playful fancies, and partly of such serious ones as I could well command.'

No sooner had Agathon ceased than a loud murmur of applause arose from all present, so becomingly had the fair youth spoken, both in praise of the God and in extenuation of himself. Then Socrates, addressing Eryximachus, said, 'Was not my fear reasonable, son of Acumenius? Did I not divine what has, in fact, happened,—that Agathon's discourse would be so wonderfully beautiful as to pre-occupy all interest in what I should say?'—'You, indeed, divined well so far, O Socrates,' said Eryximachus, 'that Agathon would speak eloquently, but not that, therefore, you would be reduced to any difficulty.' — 'How, my good friend, can I or any one else be otherwise than reduced to difficulty, who speak after a discourse so various and so eloquent, and which otherwise had been sufficiently wonderful, if, at the conclusion, the splendour of the sentences and the choice selection of the expressions had not struck all the hearers with astonishment? so that I, who well know that I can never say anything nearly so beautiful as this, would, if there had been any escape, have run away for shame. The story of Gorgias came into my mind, and I was afraid lest in reality I should suffer what Homer describes; and lest Agathon, scanning my discourse with the head of the eloquent Gorgias, should turn me to stone for speechlessness. I immediately perceived how ridiculously I had engaged myself with you to assume a part in rendering praise to Love, and had boasted that I was well skilled in amatory matters, being so ignorant of the manner in which it is becoming to render him honour, as I now perceive myself to be. I, in my simplicity, imagined that the truth ought to be spoken concerning each of the topics of our praise, and that it would be sufficient, choosing those which are the most honourable to the God, to place them in as luminous an arrangement as we could. I had, therefore, great hopes that I should speak satisfactorily, being well aware that I was acquainted with the true foundations of the praise which we have engaged to render. But since, as it appears, our purpose has been, not to render Love his due honour, but to accumulate the most beautiful and the greatest attributes of his divinity, whether they in truth belong to it or not, and that the proposed question is not how

Love ought to be praised, but how we should praise him most eloquently, my attempt must of necessity fail. It is on this account, I imagine, that in your discourses you have attributed everything to Love, and have described him to be the author of such and so great effects as, to those who are ignorant of his true nature, may exhibit him as the most beautiful and the best of all things. Not, indeed, to those who know the truth. Such praise has a splendid and imposing effect, but as I am unacquainted with the art of rendering it, my mind, which could not foresee what would be required of me, absolves me from that which my tongue promised. Farewell, then, for such praise I can never render.

'But if you desire, I will speak what I feel to be true; and that I may not expose myself to ridicule, I entreat you to consider that I speak without entering into competition with those who have preceded me. Consider, then, Phædrus, whether you will exact from me such a discourse, containing the mere truth with respect to Love, and composed of such unpremeditated expressions as may chance to offer themselves to my mind.'—Phædrus and the rest bade him speak in the manner which he judged most befitting.—'Permit me, then, O Phædrus, to ask Agathon a few questions, so that, confirmed by his agreement with me, I may proceed.' —'Willingly,' replied Phædrus, 'ask.' —Then Socrates thus began:—

'I applaud, dear Agathon, the beginning of your discourse, where you say we ought first to define and declare what Love is, and then his works. This rule I particularly approve. But, come, since you have given us a discourse of such beauty and majesty concerning Love, you are able, I doubt not, to explain this question, whether Love is the love of something or nothing? I do not ask you of what parents Love is; for the inquiry, of whether Love is the love of any father or mother, would be sufficiently ridiculous. But if I were asking you to describe that which a father is, I should ask, not whether a father was the love of any one, but whether a father was the father of any one or not; you would undoubtedly reply, that a father was the father of a son or daughter; would you not?'—'Assuredly.'—'You would define a mother in the same manner?'—'Without doubt.'—'Yet bear with me, and answer a few more questions, for I would learn from you that which I wish to know. If I should inquire, in addition, is not a brother, through the very nature of his relation, the brother of some one?'—'Certainly.'—'Of a brother or sister, is he not?' —'Without question.'—'Try to explain to me, then, the nature of Love; Love is the love of something or nothing?'—'Of something, certainly.' 'Observe and remember this concession. Tell me yet farther whether Love desires that of which it is the Love or not?'—'It desires it, assuredly.'— 'Whether, possessing that which it desires and loves, or not possessing it, does it desire and love?'—'Not possessing it, I should imagine.'—'Observe now, whether it does not appear that, of necessity, desire desires that which it wants and does not possess, and no longer desires that which it no longer wants: this appears to me, Agathon, of necessity to be; how does it appear to you?'—'It appears so to me also.'—'Would any one who was already illustrious desire to be illustrious? would any one already strong desire to be strong? From what has already been conceded, it follows that he would not. If any one already strong should desire to be strong; or any one already swift should desire to be swift; or any one already healthy should desire to be healthy, it must be concluded that they still desired the advantages of which they already seemed possessed. To destroy the foundation of this error, observe, Agathon, that each of these persons must possess the several advantages in question, at the moment present to our thoughts, whether he will or no. And now, is it possible that those advantages should be at that time the objects of his desire? For, if any one should say, being in health, "I desire to be in health;" being rich, "I desire to be rich, and thus still desire those things which I already possess," we might say to him, "You, my friend, possess health, and strength, and riches; you do not desire to possess now, but to continue to possess them in future; for, whether you will or no, they now belong to you. Consider, then, whether, when you say that you desire things present to you, and in your own possession, you say anything else than that you desire the advantages to be for the future also in your possession." What else could he reply?' —'Nothing, indeed.'—'Is not Love, then, the love of that which is not within its reach, and which cannot hold in security, for the future, those things of which it obtains a present and transitory possession?'—'Evidently.' —'Love, therefore, and everything else that desires anything, desires that which is absent and beyond his reach, that which it has not, that which is not itself, that which it wants; such are the things of which there are desire and love.'—'Assuredly.'

'Come,' said Socrates, 'let us review your concessions. Is Love anything else than the love first of something; and, secondly, of those things of which it has need?'—'Nothing.'—'Now, remember of those things you said in your discourse, that Love was the love —if you wish I will remind you. I think you said something of this kind, that all the affairs of the gods were admirably disposed through the love of the things which are beautiful; for there was no love of things deformed; did you not say so?'—'I confess that I did.'—'You said what was most likely to be true, my friend; and if the matter be so, the love of beauty must be one thing, and the love of deformity another.'—'Certainly.'—'It is conceded, then, that Love loves that which he wants, but possesses not?'—'Yes, certainly.'—'But Love wants and does not possess beauty?'—'Indeed it must necessarily follow.'—'What, then! call you that beautiful which has need of beauty and possesses not?'—'Assuredly no.'—'Do you still assert, then, that Love is beautiful, if all that we have said be true?'—'Indeed, Socrates,' said Agathon, 'I am in danger of being convicted of ignorance, with respect to all that I then spoke.'—'You spoke most eloquently, my dear Agathon; but bear with my questions yet a moment. You admit that things which are good are also beautiful?'—'No doubt.' —'If Love, then, be in want of beautiful things, and things which are good are beautiful, he must be in want of things which are good?'—'I cannot refute your arguments, Socrates.'—'You cannot refute truth, my dear Agathon: to refute Socrates is nothing difficult.

'But I will dismiss these questionings. At present let me endeavour, to the best of my power, to repeat to you, on the basis of the points which have been agreed upon between me and Agathon, a discourse concerning Love which I formerly heard from the prophetess Diotima, who was profoundly skilled in this and many other doctrines, and who, ten years before the pestilence, procured to the Athenians, through their sacrifices, a delay of the disease; for it was she who taught me the science of things relating to Love.

'As you well remarked, Agathon, we ought to declare who and what is Love, and then his works. It is easiest to relate them in the same order as the foreign prophetess observed when, questioning me, she related them. For I said to her much the same things that Agathon has just said to me—that Love was a great deity, and that he was beautiful; and she refuted me with the same reasons as I have employed to refute Agathon, compelling me to infer that he was neither beautiful nor good, as I said.—"What, then," I objected, "O Diotima, is Love ugly and evil?"—"Good words, I entreat you," said Diotima; "do you think that everything which is not beautiful must of necessity be ugly?"—"Certainly."—"And everything that is not wise, ignorant? Do you not perceive that there is something between ignorance and wisdom?"—"What is that?"—"To have a right opinion or conjecture. Observe, that this kind of opinion, for which no reason can be rendered, cannot be called knowledge; for how can that be called knowledge which is without evidence or reason? Nor ignorance, on the other hand; for how can that be called ignorance which arrives at the persuasion of that which it really is? A right opinion is something between understanding and ignorance."—I confessed that what she alleged was true.—"Do not then say," she continued, "that what is not beautiful is of necessity deformed, nor what is not good is of necessity evil; nor, since you have confessed that Love is neither beautiful nor good, infer, therefore, that he is deformed or evil, but rather something intermediate."

'"But," I said, "Love is confessed by all to be a great God."—"Do you mean, when you say all, all those who know, or those who know not, what they say?"—"All collectively."—"And how can that be, Socrates?" said she, laughing; "how can he be acknowledged to be a great God by those who assert that he is not even a God at all?"—"And who are they?" I said.—"You for one, and I for another."—"How can you say that, Diotima?"—"Easily," she replied, "and with truth; for tell me, do you not own that all the Gods are beautiful and happy? or will you presume to maintain that any

God is otherwise?"—"By Jupiter, not I!"—"Do you not call those alone happy who possess all things that are beautiful and good?"—"Certainly." —"You have confessed that Love, through his desire for things beautiful and good, possesses not those materials of happiness."—"Indeed, such was my concession."—"But how can we conceive a God to be without the possession of what is beautiful and good?" —"In no manner, I confess."—"Observe, then, that you do not consider Love to be a God."—"What, then," I said, "is Love a mortal?"—"By no means."—"But what, then?"—"Like those things which I have before instanced, he is neither mortal nor immortal, but something intermediate." —"What is that, O Diotima?"— "A great dæmon, Socrates; and everything dæmoniacal holds an intermediate place between what is divine and what is mortal."

'"What is his power and nature?" I inquired.—"He interprets and makes a communication between divine and human things, conveying the prayers and sacrifices of men to the Gods, and communicating the commands and directions concerning the mode of worship most pleasing to them, from Gods to men. He fills up that intermediate space between these two classes of beings, so as to bind together, by his own power, the whole universe of things. Through him subsist all divination, and the science of sacred things as it relates to sacrifices, and expiations, and disenchantments, and prophecy, and magic. The divine nature cannot immediately communicate with what is human, but all that intercourse and converse which is conceded by the Gods to men, both whilst they sleep and when they wake, subsists through the intervention of Love; and he who is wise in the science of this intercourse is supremely happy, and participates in the dæmoniacal nature; whilst he who is wise in any other science or art remains a mere ordinary slave. These dæmons are, indeed, many and various, and one of them is Love."

'"Who are the parents of Love?" I inquired.—"The history of what you ask," replied Diotima, "is somewhat long; nevertheless I will explain it to you. On the birth of Venus the Gods celebrated a great feast, and among them came Plenty, the son of Metis. After supper, Poverty, observing the profusion, came to beg, and stood beside the door. Plenty being drunk with nectar, for wine was not yet invented, went out into Jupiter's garden, and fell into a deep sleep. Poverty wishing to have a child by Plenty, on account of her low estate, lay down by him, and from his embraces conceived Love. Love is, therefore, the follower and servant of Venus, because he was conceived at her birth, and because by nature he is a lover of all that is beautiful, and Venus was beautiful. And since Love is the child of Poverty and Plenty, his nature and fortune participate in that of his parents. He is for ever poor, and so far from being delicate and beautiful, as mankind imagine, he is squalid and withered; he flies low along the ground, and is homeless and unsandalled; he sleeps without covering before the doors, and in the unsheltered streets; possessing thus far his mother's nature, that he is ever the companion of Want. But, inasmuch as he participates in that of his father, he is for ever scheming to obtain things which are good and beautiful; he is fearless, vehement, and strong; a dreadful hunter, for ever weaving some new contrivance; exceedingly cautious and prudent, and full of resources; he is also, during his whole existence, a philosopher, a powerful enchanter, a wizard, and a subtle sophist. And, as his nature is neither mortal nor immortal, on the same day when he is fortunate and successful, he will at one time flourish, and then die away, and then, according to his father's nature, again revive. All that he acquires perpetually flows away from him, so that Love is never either rich or poor, and holding for ever an intermediate state between ignorance and wisdom. The case stands thus:—No God philosophizes or desires to become wise, for he is wise; nor, if there exist any other being who is wise, does he philosophize. Nor do the ignorant philosophize, for they desire not to become wise; for this is the evil of ignorance, that he who has neither intelligence, nor virtue, nor delicacy of sentiment, imagines that he possesses all those things sufficiently. He seeks not, therefore, that possession, of whose want he is not aware."—"Who, then, O Diotima," I inquired, "are philosophers, if they are neither the ignorant nor the wise?"—"It is evident, even to a child, that they are those intermediate persons, among whom is Love. For Wisdom is one of the most beautiful of all things; Love is that which thirsts for the beautiful, so that Love is of necessity a philosopher, philosophy being an intermediate state between ignorance and wisdom. His parentage accounts for his condition, being the child of a wise and well-provided father, and of a mother both ignorant and poor.

'"Such is the dæmoniacal nature, my dear Socrates; nor do I wonder at your error concerning Love, for you thought, as I conjecture from what you say, that Love was not the lover but the beloved, and thence well concluded that he must be supremely beautiful; for that which is the object of Love must indeed be fair, and delicate, and perfect, and most happy; but Love inherits, as I have declared, a totally opposite nature."—"Your words have persuasion in them O stranger," I said; "be it as you say

But this Love, what advantages does he afford to men?"—"I will proceed to explain it to you, Socrates. Love, being such and so produced as I have described, is, indeed, as you say, the love of things which are beautiful. But if any one should ask us, saying: O Socrates and Diotima, why is Love the love of beautiful things? Or, in plainer words, what does the lover of that which is beautiful, love in the object of his love, and seek from it?"—"He seeks," I said, interrupting her, "the property and possession of it."—"But that," she replied, "might still be met with another question, What has he, who possesses that which is beautiful?" —"Indeed, I cannot immediately reply."—"But if, changing the beautiful for good, any one should inquire, —I ask, O Socrates, what is that which he who loves that which is good, loves in the object of his love?"—"To be in his possession," I replied.—"And what has he, who has the possession of good?" —"This question is of easier solution: he is happy."—"Those who are happy, then, are happy through the possession; and it is useless to inquire what he desires, who desires to be happy; the question seems to have a complete reply. But do you think that this wish and this love are common to all men, and that all desire that that which is good should be for ever present to them?"—"Certainly, common to all." —"Why do we not say, then, Socrates, that every one loves? if, indeed, all love perpetually the same thing? But we say that some love, and some do not."—"Indeed, I wonder why it is so." —"Wonder not," said Diotima, "for we select a particular species of love, and apply to it distinctively the appellation of that which is universal."

'"Give me an example of such a select application."—"Poetry; which is a general name signifying every cause whereby anything proceeds from that which is not, into that which is; so that the exercise of every inventive art is poetry, and all such artists poets. Yet they are not called poets, but distinguished by other names; and one portion or species of poetry, that which has relation to music and rhythm, is divided from all others, and known by the name belonging to all. For this is alone properly called poetry, and those who exercise the art of this species of poetry, poets. So with respect to Love. Love is indeed universally all that earnest desire for the possession of happiness and that which is good; the greatest and the subtlest love, and which inhabits the heart of every living being; but those who seek this object through the acquirement of wealth, or the exercise of the gymnastic arts, or philosophy, are not said to love, nor are called lovers; one species alone is called love, and those alone are said to be lovers, and to love, who seek the attainment of the universal desire through one species of love, which is peculiarly distinguished by the name belonging to the whole. It is asserted by some that they love who are seeking the lost half of their divided being. But I assert that Love is neither the love of half nor of the whole, unless, my friend, it meets with that which is good; since men willingly cut off their own hands and feet, if they think that they are the cause of evil to them. Nor do they cherish and embrace that which may belong to themselves merely because it is their own, unless, indeed, any one should choose to say that that which is good is attached to his own nature and is his own, whilst that which is evil is foreign and accidental; but love nothing but that which is good. Does it not appear so to you?"—"Assuredly."—"Can we, then, simply affirm that men love that which is good?"—"Without doubt."—"What, then, must we not add, that, in addition to loving that which is good, they love that it should be present to themselves?"—"Indeed that must be added."—"And not merely that it should be present, but that it should ever be present?"—"This also must be added."

'"Love, then, is collectively the desire

in men that good should be for ever present to them."—"Most true."—"Since this is the general definition of Love, can you explain in what mode of attaining its object, and in what species of actions, does Love peculiarly consist?"—"If I knew what you ask, O Diotima, I should not have so much wondered at your wisdom, nor have sought you out for the purpose of deriving improvement from your instructions."—"I will tell you," she replied: "Love is the desire of generation in the beautiful, both with relation to the body and the soul."—"I must be a diviner to comprehend what you say, for, being such as I am, I confess that I do not understand it."—"But I will explain it more clearly. The bodies and the souls of all human beings are alike pregnant with their future progeny, and when we arrive at a certain age our nature impels us to bring forth and propagate. This nature is unable to produce in that which is deformed, but it can produce in that which is beautiful. The intercourse of the male and female in generation, a divine work, through pregnancy and production, is, as it were, something immortal in mortality. These things cannot take place in that which is incongruous; for that which is deformed is incongruous, but that which is beautiful is congruous with what is immortal and divine. Beauty is, therefore, the fate and the Juno Lucina to generation. Wherefore, whenever that which is pregnant with the generative principle approaches that which is beautiful, it becomes transported with delight, and is poured forth in overflowing pleasure, and propagates. But when it approaches that which is deformed, it is contracted by sadness, and, being repelled and checked, it does not produce, but retains unwillingly that with which it is pregnant. Wherefore, to one pregnant, and, as it were, already bursting with the load of his desire, the impulse towards that which is beautiful is intense, on account of the great pain of retaining that which he has conceived. Love, then, O Socrates, is not as you imagine the love of the beautiful."—"What, then?" —"Of generation and production in the beautiful."—"Why then of generation?"—"Generation is something eternal and immortal in mortality. It necessarily, from what has been confessed, follows, that we must desire immortality together with what is good, since Love is the desire that good be for ever present to us. Of necessity Love must also be the desire of immortality."

'Diotima taught me all this doctrine in the discourse we had together concerning Love; and in addition she inquired, "What do you think, Socrates, is the cause of this love and desire? Do you not perceive how all animals, both those of the earth and of the air, are affected when they desire the propagation of their species, affected even to weakness and disease by the impulse of their love; first, longing to be mixed with each other, and then seeking nourishment for their offspring, so that the feeblest are ready to contend with the strongest in obedience to this law, and to die for the sake of their young, or to waste away with hunger, and do or suffer anything so that they may not want nourishment. It might be said that human beings do these things through reason, but can you explain why other animals are thus affected through love?"—I confessed that I did not know.—"Do you imagine yourself," said she, "to be skilful in the science of Love, if you are ignorant of these things?"—"As I said before, O Diotima, I come to you, well knowing how much I am in need of a teacher. But explain to me, I entreat you, the cause of these things, and of the other things relating to Love."—"If," said Diotima, "you believe that Love is of the same nature as we have mutually agreed upon, wonder not that such are its effects. For the mortal nature seeks, so far as it is able, to become deathless and eternal. But it can only accomplish this desire by generation, which for ever leaves another new in place of the old. For, although each human being be severally said to live, and be the same from youth to old age, yet that which is called the same never contains within itself the same things, but always is becoming new by the loss and change of that which it possessed before; both the hair, and the flesh, and the bones, and the entire body.

'"And not only does this change take place in the body, but also with respect to the soul. Manners, morals, opinions, desires, pleasures, sorrows, fears; none of these ever remain unchanged in the same persons, but some die away, and others are produced. And, what is yet more strange is, that not only does some knowledge spring up, and another decay, and that we are never the same with respect to our knowledge, but that each several object of our thoughts suffers the same revolution. That which is called meditation, or the exercise of memory, is the science of the escape or departure of memory; for, forgetfulness is the going out of knowledge; and meditation, calling up a new memory in the place of that which has departed, preserves knowledge; so that, though for ever displaced and restored, it seems to be the same. In this manner everything mortal is preserved: not that it is constant and eternal, like that which is divine, but that in the place of what has grown old and is departed, it leaves another new like that which it was itself. By this contrivance, O Socrates, does what is mortal, the body and all other things, partake of immortality; that which is immortal is immortal in another manner. Wonder not, then, if everything by nature cherishes that which was produced from itself, for this earnest Love is a tendency towards eternity."

'Having heard this discourse, I was astonished, and asked, "Can these things be true, O wisest Diotima?" And she, like an accomplished sophist, said, "Know well, O Socrates, that if you only regard that love of glory which inspires men, you will wonder at your own unskilfulness in not having discovered all that I now declare. Observe with how vehement a desire they are affected to become illustrious and to prolong their glory into immortal time, to obtain which object, far more ardently than for the sake of their children, all men are ready to engage in many dangers, and expend their fortunes, and submit to any labours and incur any death. Do you believe that Alcestis would have died in the place of Admetus, or Achilles for the revenge of Patroclus, or Codrus for the kingdom of his posterity, if they had not believed that the immortal memory of their actions, which we now cherish, would have remained after their death? Far otherwise; all such deeds are done for the sake of ever-living virtue, and this immortal glory which they have obtained; and inasmuch as any one is of an excellent nature, so much the more is he impelled to attain this reward. For they love what is immortal.

'"Those whose bodies alone are pregnant with this principle of immortality are attracted by women, seeking through the production of children what they imagine to be happiness and immortality and an enduring remembrance; but they whose souls are far more pregnant than their bodies, conceive and produce that which is more suitable to the soul. What is suitable to the soul? Intelligence and every other power and excellence of the mind; of which all poets, and all other artists who are creative and inventive, are the authors. The greatest and most admirable wisdom is that which regulates the government of families and states, and which is called moderation and justice. Whosoever, therefore, from his youth feels his soul pregnant with the conception of these excellences, is divine; and when due time arrives, desires to bring forth; and wandering about, he seeks the beautiful in which he may propagate what he has conceived; for there is no generation in that which is deformed; he embraces those bodies which are beautiful rather than those which are deformed, in obedience to the principle which is within him, which is ever seeking to perpetuate itself. And if he meets, in conjunction with loveliness of form, a beautiful, generous, and gentle soul, he embraces both at once, and immediately undertakes to educate this object of his love, and is inspired with an overflowing persuasion to declare what is virtue, and what he ought to be who would attain to its possession, and what are the duties which it exacts. For, by the intercourse with, and as it were, the very touch of that which is beautiful, he brings forth and produces what he had formerly conceived; and nourishes and educates that which is thus produced together with the object of his love, whose image, whether absent or present, is never divided from his mind.

So that those who are thus united are linked by a nobler community and a firmer love, as being the common parents of a lovelier and more endearing progeny than the parents of other children. And every one who considers what posterity Homer and Hesiod and the other great poets have left behind them, the sources of their own immortal memory and renown, or what children of his soul Lycurgus has appointed to be the guardians, not only of Lacedæmon, but of all Greece; or what an illustrious progeny of laws Solon has produced, and how many admirable achievements, both among the Greeks and Barbarians, men have left as the pledges of that love which subsisted between them and the beautiful, would choose rather to be the parent of such children than those in a human shape.

For divine honours have often been rendered to them on account of such children, but on account of those in human shape, never.

'"Your own meditation, O Socrates, might perhaps have initiated you in all these things which I have already taught you on the subject of Love. But those perfect and sublime ends to which these are only the means, I know not that you would have been competent to discover. I will declare them, therefore, and will render them as intelligible as possible: do you meanwhile strain all your attention to trace the obscure depth of the subject. He who aspires to love rightly, ought from his earliest youth to seek an intercourse with beautiful forms, and first to make a single form the object of his love, and therein to generate intellectual excellences. He ought, then, to consider that beauty in whatever form it resides is the brother of that beauty which subsists in another form; and if he ought to pursue that which is beautiful in form, it would be absurd to imagine that beauty is not one and the same thing in all forms, and would therefore remit much of his ardent preference towards one, through his perception of the multitude of claims upon his love. In addition, he would consider the beauty which is in souls more excellent than that which is in form. So that one endowed with an admirable soul, even though the flower of the form were withered, would suffice him as the object of his love and care, and the companion with whom he might seek and produce such conclusions as tend to the improvement of youth; so that it might be led to observe the beauty and the conformity which there is in the observation of its duties and the laws, and to esteem little the mere beauty of the outward form. He would then conduct his pupil to science, so that he might look upon the loveliness of wisdom; and that contemplating thus the universal beauty, no longer would he unworthily and meanly enslave himself to the attractions of one form in love, nor one subject of discipline or science, but would turn towards the wide ocean of intellectual beauty, and from the sight of the lovely and majestic forms which it contains, would abundantly bring forth his conceptions in philosophy; until, strengthened and confirmed, he should at length steadily contemplate one science, which is the science of this universal beauty.

'"Attempt, I entreat you, to mark what I say with as keen an observation as you can. He who has been disciplined to this point in Love, by contemplating beautiful objects gradually, and in their order, now arriving at the end of all that concerns Love, on a sudden beholds a beauty wonderful in its nature. This is it, O Socrates, for the sake of which all the former labours were endured. It is eternal, unproduced, indestructible; neither subject to increase nor decay: not, like other things, partly beautiful and partly deformed; not at one time beautiful and at another time not; not beautiful in relation to one thing and deformed in relation to another; not here beautiful and there deformed; not beautiful in the estimation of one person and deformed in that of another; nor can this supreme beauty be figured to the imagination like a beautiful face, or beautiful hands, or any portion of the body, nor like any discourse, nor any science. Nor does it subsist in any other that lives or is, either in earth, or in heaven, or in any other place; but it is eternally uniform and consistent, and monoeidic with itself. All other things are beautiful through a participation of it, with this condition, that although they are subject to production and decay, it never becomes more or less, or endures any change. When any one, ascending from a correct system of Love, begins to contemplate this supreme beauty, he already touches the consummation of his labour. For such as discipline themselves upon this system, or are conducted by another beginning to ascend through these transitory objects which

are beautiful, towards that which is beauty itself, proceeding as on steps from the love of one form to that of two, and from that of two to that of all forms which are beautiful; and from beautiful forms to beautiful habits and institutions, and from institutions to beautiful doctrines; until, from the meditation of many doctrines, they arrive at that which is nothing else than the doctrine of the supreme beauty itself, in the knowledge and contemplation of which at length they repose.
'"Such a life as this, my dear Socrates," exclaimed the stranger Prophetess, "spent in the contemplation of the beautiful, is the life for men to live; which if you chance ever to experience, you will esteem far beyond gold and rich garments, and even those lovely persons whom you and many others

now gaze on with astonishment, and are prepared neither to eat nor drink so that you may behold and live for ever with these objects of your love! What then shall we imagine to be the aspect of the supreme beauty itself, simple, pure, uncontaminated with the intermixture of human flesh and colours, and all other idle and unreal shapes attendant on mortality; the divine, the original, the supreme, the monoeidic beautiful itself? What must be the life of him who dwells with and gazes on that which it becomes us all to seek? Think you not that to him alone is accorded the prerogative of bringing forth, not images and shadows of virtue, for he is in contact not with a shadow but with reality; with virtue itself, in the production and nourishment of which he becomes dear to the Gods, and if such a privilege is conceded to any human being, himself immortal."

'Such, O Phædrus, and my other friends, was what Diotima said. And being persuaded by her words, I have since occupied myself in attempting to persuade others, that it is not easy to find a better assistant than Love in seeking to communicate immortality to our human natures. Wherefore I exhort every one to honour Love; I hold him in honour, and chiefly exercise myself in amatory matters, and exhort others to do so; and now and ever do I praise the power and excellence of Love, in the best manner that I can. Let this discourse, if it pleases you, Phædrus, be considered as an encomium of Love; or call it by what other name you will.'

The whole assembly praised his discourse, and Aristophanes was on the point of making some remarks on the allusion made by Socrates to him in a part of his discourse, when suddenly they heard a loud knocking at the door of the vestibule, and a clamour as of revellers, attended by a flute-player.—'Go, boys,' said Agathon, 'and see who is there: if they are any of our friends, call them in; if not, say that we have already done drinking.'—A minute afterwards they heard the voice of Alcibiades in the vestibule excessively drunk and roaring out:—'Where is Agathon? Lead me to Agathon!'—The flute-player and some of his companions then led him in, and placed him against the door-post, crowned with a thick crown of ivy and violets, and having a quantity of fillets on his head.—'My friends,' he cried out, 'hail! I am excessively drunk already, but I'll drink with you, if you will. If not, we will go away after having crowned Agathon, for which purpose I came. I assure you that I could not come yesterday, but I am now here with these fillets round my temples, that from my own head I may crown his who, with your leave, is the most beautiful and wisest of men. Are you laughing at me because I am drunk? Ay, I know what I say is true, whether you laugh or not. But tell me at once, whether I shall come in, or no. Will you drink with me?'

Agathon and the whole party desired him to come in, and recline among them; so he came in, led by his companions. He then unbound his fillets that he might crown Agathon, and though Socrates was just before his eyes, he did not see him, but sat down by Agathon, between Socrates and him, for Socrates moved out of the way to make room for him. When he sat down, he embraced Agathon and crowned him; and Agathon desired the slaves to untie his sandals, that he might make a third, and recline on the same couch. 'By all means,' said Alcibiades, 'but what third companion have we here?' And at the same time turning round and seeing Socrates, he leaped up and cried out:—'O Hercules! what have we here? You, Socrates, lying in ambush for me wherever I go! and meeting me just as you always do, when I least expected to see you! And now, what are you come here for? Why have you chosen to recline exactly in this place, and not near Aristophanes, or any one else who is or wishes to be ridiculous, but have contrived to take your place beside the most delightful person of the whole party?'—'Agathon,' said Socrates, 'see if you cannot defend me. I declare my friendship for this man is a bad business; from the moment that I first began to know him I have never been permitted to converse with, or so much as to look upon any one else. If I do, he is so jealous and suspicious that he does the most extravagant things, and hardly refrains from beating me. I entreat you to prevent him from doing anything of that kind at present. Procure a reconciliation: or, if he perseveres in attempting any violence, I entreat you to defend me.'—'Indeed,' said Alcibiades, 'I will not be reconciled to you; I shall find another opportunity to punish you for this. But now,' said he, addressing Agathon, 'lend me some of those fillets, that I may crown the wonderful head of this fellow, lest I incur the blame, that having crowned you, I neglected to crown him who conquers all men with his discourses, not yesterday alone, as you did, but ever.'

Saying this he took the fillets, and having bound the head of Socrates, and again having reclined, said:—'Come, my friends, you seem to be sober enough. You must not flinch, but drink, for that was your agreement with me before I came in. I choose as president, until you have drunk enough—myself. Come, Agathon, if you have got a great goblet, fetch it out. But no matter, that wine cooler will do; bring it, boy!' And observing that it held more than eight cups, he first drank it off, and then ordered it to be filled for Socrates, and said:—'Observe, my friends, I cannot invent any scheme against Socrates, for he will drink as much as any one desires him, and not be in the least drunk.' Socrates, after the boy had filled up, drank it off; and Eryximachus said:—'Shall we then have no conversation or singing over our cups, but drink down stupidly, just as if we were thirsty?' And Alcibiades said:— 'Ah, Eryximachus, I did not see you before; hail, you excellent son of a wise and excellent father!'—'Hail to you also,' replied Eryximachus, 'but what shall we do?'—'Whatever you command, for we ought to submit to your directions; a physician is worth a hundred common men. Command us as you please.'—'Listen then,' said Eryximachus; 'before you came in, each of us had agreed to deliver as eloquent a discourse as he could in praise of Love, beginning at the right hand; all the rest of us have fulfilled our engagement; you have not spoken, and yet have drunk with us; you ought to bear your part in the discussion; and having done so, command what you please to Socrates, who shall have the privilege of doing so to his right-hand neighbour, and so on to the others.'—'Indeed, there appears some justice in your proposal, Eryximachus, though it is rather unfair to induce a drunken man to set his discourse in competition with that of those who are sober. And, besides, did Socrates really persuade you that what he just said about me was true, or do you not know that matters are in fact exactly the reverse of his representation? For I seriously believe that, should

I praise in his presence, be he god or man, any other beside himself, he would not keep his hands off me. But I assure you, Socrates, I will praise no one beside yourself, in your presence.'
'Do so, then,' said Eryximachus; 'praise Socrates if you please.'—'What!' said Alcibiades, 'shall I attack him, and punish him before you all?'—'What have you got into your head now,' said Socrates; are you going to expose me to ridicule, and to misrepresent me? Or what are you going to do?'—'I will only speak the truth; will you permit me on this condition?'—'I not only permit, but exhort you to say all the truth you know,' replied Socrates.—'I obey you willingly,' said Alcibiades; 'and if I advance anything untrue, do you, if you please, interrupt me, and convict me of misrepresentation, for I would

never willingly speak falsely. And bear with me if I do not relate things in their order, but just as I remember them, for it is not easy for a man in my present condition to enumerate systematically all your singularities.

'I will begin the praise of Socrates by comparing him to a certain statue. Perhaps he will think that this statue is introduced for the sake of ridicule, but I assure you that it is necessary for the illustration of truth. I assert, then, that Socrates is exactly like those Silenuses that sit in the sculptors' shops, and which are carved holding flutes or pipes, but which, when divided in two, are found to contain withinside the images of the gods. I assert that Socrates is like the satyr Marsyas. That your form and appearance are like these satyrs, I think that even you will not venture to deny; and how like you are to them in all other things, now hear. Are you not scornful and petulant? If you deny this, I will bring witnesses. Are you not a piper, and far more wonderful a one than he? For Marsyas, and whoever now pipes the music that he taught, for that music which is of heaven, and described as being taught by Marsyas, enchants men through the power of the mouth. For if any musician, be he skilful or not, awakens this music, it alone enables him to retain the minds of men, and from the divinity of its nature makes evident those who are in want of the Gods and initiation. You differ only from Marsyas in this circumstance, that you effect without instruments, by mere words, all that he can do. For when we hear Pericles, or any other accomplished orator, deliver a discourse, no one, as it were, cares anything about it. But when any one hears you, or even your words related by another, though ever so rude and unskilful a speaker, be that person a woman, man, or child, we are struck and retained, as it were, by the discourse clinging to our mind.

'If I was not afraid that I am a great deal too drunk, I would confirm to you by an oath the strange effects which I assure you I have suffered from his words, and suffer still; for when I hear him speak, my heart leaps up far more than the hearts of those who celebrate the Corybantic mysteries: my tears are poured out as he talks, a thing I have seen happen to many others beside myself. I have heard Pericles and other excellent orators, and have been pleased with their discourses, but I suffered nothing of this kind; nor was my soul ever on those occasions disturbed and filled with self-reproach, as if it were slavishly laid prostrate. But this Marsyas here has often affected me in the way I describe, until the life which I lead seemed hardly worth living. Do not deny it, Socrates; for I well know that if even now I chose to listen to you, I could not resist, but should again suffer the same effects. For, my friends, he forces me to confess that while I myself am still in want of many things, I neglect my own necessities, and attend to those of the Athenians. I stop my ears, therefore, as from the Syrens, and flee away as fast as possible, that I may not sit down beside him and grow old in listening to his talk. For this man has reduced me to feel the sentiment of shame, which I imagine no one would readily believe was in me; he alone inspires me with remorse and awe. For I feel in his presence my incapacity of refuting what he says, or of refusing to do that which he directs; but when I depart from him, the glory which the multitude confers overwhelms me. I escape, therefore, and hide myself from him, and when I see him I am overwhelmed with humiliation, because I have neglected to do what I have confessed to him ought to be done; and often and often have I wished that he were no longer to be seen among men. But if that were to happen, I well know that I should suffer far greater pain; so that where I can turn, or what I can do with this man, I know not. All this have I and many others suffered from the pipings of this satyr.

'And observe how like he is to what I said, and what a wonderful power he possesses. Know that there is not one of you who is aware of the real nature of Socrates; but since I have begun, I will make him plain to you. You observe how passionately Socrates affects the intimacy of those who are beautiful, and how ignorant he professes himself to be; appearances in themselves excessively Silenic. This, my friends, is the external form with which, like one of the sculptured Sileni, he has clothed himself; for if you open him, you will find within admirable temperance and wisdom. For he cares not for mere beauty, but despises more than any one can imagine all external possessions, whether it be beauty, or wealth, or glory, or any other thing for which the multitude felicitates the possessor.

He esteems these things and us who honour them, as nothing, and lives among men, making all the objects of their admiration the playthings of his irony. But I know not if any one of you have ever seen the divine images which are within, when he has been opened and is serious. I have seen them, and they are so supremely beautiful, so golden, so divine, and wonderful, that everything which Socrates commands surely ought to be obeyed, even like the voice of a God.

'At one time we were fellow-soldiers, and had our mess together in the camp before Potidæa. Socrates there overcame not only me, but every one beside, in endurance of toils: when, as often happens in a campaign, we were reduced to few provisions, there were none who could sustain hunger like

Socrates; and when we had plenty, he alone seemed to enjoy our military fare. He never drank much willingly, but when he was compelled, he conquered all even in that to which he was least accustomed; and what is most astonishing, no person ever saw Socrates drunk either then or at any other time. In the depth of winter (and the winters there are excessively rigid) he sustained calmly incredible hardships: and amongst other things, whilst the frost was intolerably severe, and no one went out of their tents, or if they went out, wrapt themselves up carefully, and put fleeces under their feet, and bound their legs with hairy skins, Socrates went out only with the same cloak on that he usually wore, and walked barefoot upon the ice; more easily, indeed, than those who had sandalled themselves so delicately: so that the soldiers thought that he did it to mock their want of fortitude. It would indeed be worth while to commemorate all that this brave man did and endured in that expedition. In one instance he was seen early in the morning standing in one place wrapt in meditation; and as he seemed not to be able to unravel the subject of his thoughts, he still continued to stand as inquiring and discussing within himself, and when noon came, the soldiers observed him, and said to one another — "Socrates has been standing there thinking, ever since the morning." At last some Ionians came to the spot, and having supped, as it was summer, bringing their blankets, they lay down to sleep in the cool; they observed that Socrates continued to stand there the whole night until morning, and that, when the sun rose, he saluted it with a prayer and departed.

'I ought not to omit what Socrates is in battle. For in that battle after which the generals decreed to me the prize of courage, Socrates alone of all men was the saviour of my life, standing by me when I had fallen and was wounded, and preserving both myself and my arms from the hands of the enemy. On that occasion I entreated the generals to decree the prize, as it was most due, to him. And this, O Socrates, you cannot deny, that while the generals, wishing to conciliate a person of my rank, desired to give me the prize, you were far more earnestly desirous than the generals that this glory should be attributed not to yourself, but me.

'But to see Socrates when our army was

defeated and scattered in flight at Delium, was a spectacle worthy to behold. On that occasion I was among the cavalry, and he on foot, heavily armed. After the total rout of our troops, he and Laches retreated together; I came up by chance, and seeing them, bade them be of good cheer, for that I would not leave them. As I was on horseback, and therefore less occupied by a regard of my own situation, I could better observe than at Potidæa the beautiful spectacle exhibited by Socrates on this emergency. How superior was he to Laches in presence of mind and courage! Your representation of him on the stage, O Aristophanes, was not wholly unlike his real self on this occasion, for he walked and darted his regards around with a majestic composure, looking tranquilly both on his friends and enemies; so that it was evident to every one, even from afar, that whoever should venture to attack him would encounter a desperate resistance. He and his companions thus departed in safety; for those who are scattered in flight are pursued and killed, whilst men hesitate to touch those who exhibit such a countenance as that of Socrates even in defeat.

'Many other and most wonderful qualities might well be praised in Socrates; but such as these might singly be attributed to others. But that which is unparalleled in Socrates is, that he is unlike and above comparison with all other men, whether those who have lived in ancient times, or those who exist now. For it may be conjectured, that Brasidas and many others are such as was Achilles. Pericles deserves comparison with Nestor and Antenor; and other excellent persons of various times may, with probability, be drawn into comparison with each other. But to such a singular man as this, both himself and his discourses are so uncommon, no one, should he seek, would find a parallel among the present or the past generations of mankind; unless they should say that he resembled those with whom I lately compared him, for, assuredly, he and his discourses are like nothing but the Sileni and the Satyrs. At first I forgot to make you observe how like his discourses are to those Satyrs when they are opened, for, if any one will listen to the talk of Socrates, it will appear to him at first extremely ridiculous; the phrases and expressions which he employs, fold around his exterior the skin, as it were, of a rude and wanton Satyr. He is always talking about great market-asses, and brass-founders, and leather-cutters, and skin-dressers; and this is his perpetual custom, so that any dull and unobservant person might easily laugh at his discourse. But if any one should see it opened, as it were, and get within the sense of his words, he would then find that they alone of all that enters into the mind of man to utter, had a profound and persuasive meaning, and that they were most divine; and that they presented to the mind innumerable images of every excellence, and that they tended towards objects of the highest moment, or rather towards all that he who seeks the possession of what is supremely beautiful and good need regard as essential to the accomplishment of his ambition.

'These are the things, my friends, for which I praise Socrates.'

Alcibiades having said this, the whole party burst into a laugh at his frankness, and Socrates said, 'You seem to be sober enough, Alcibiades, else you would not have made such a circuit of words, only to hide the main design for which you made this long speech, and which, as it were carelessly, you just throw in at the last; now, as if you had not said all this for the mere purpose of dividing me and Agathon? You think that I ought to be your friend, and to care for no one else. I have found you out; it is evident enough for what design you invented all this Satyrical and Silenic drama. But, my dear Agathon, do not let his device succeed. I entreat you to permit no one to throw discord between us.'—'No doubt,' said

Agathon, 'he sate down between us only that he might divide us; but this shall not assist his scheme, for I will come and sit near you.'—'Do so,' said Socrates, 'come, there is room for you by me.'—'Oh Jupiter!' exclaimed Alcibiades, 'what I endure from that man! He thinks to subdue every way; but, at least, I pray you, let Agathon remain between us.'—'Impossible,' said Socrates, 'you have just praised me; I ought to praise him sitting at my right hand. If Agathon is placed beside you, will he not praise me before I praise him? Now, my dear friend, allow the young man to receive what praise I can give him. I have a great desire to pronounce his encomium.'—'Quick, quick, Alcibiades,' said Agathon, 'I cannot stay here, I must change my place, or Socrates will not praise me.'—Agathon then arose to take his place near Socrates.

He had no sooner reclined than there came in a number of revellers—for some one who had gone out had left the door open—and took their places on the vacant couches, and everything became full of confusion; and no order being observed, every one was obliged to drink a great quantity of wine. Eryximachus, and Phædrus, and some others, said Aristodemus, went home to bed; that, for his part, he went to sleep on his couch, and slept long and soundly—the nights were then long—until the cock crew in the morning. When he awoke he found that some were still fast asleep, and others had gone home, and that Aristophanes, Agathon, and Socrates had alone stood it out, and were still drinking out of a great goblet which they passed round and round. Socrates was disputing between them. The beginning of their discussion Aristodemus said that he did not recollect, because he was asleep; but it was terminated by Socrates forcing them to confess, that the same person is able to compose both tragedy and comedy, and that the foundations of the tragic and comic arts were essentially the same. They, rather convicted than convinced, went to sleep. Aristophanes first awoke, and then, it being broad daylight, Agathon. Socrates, having put them to sleep, went away, Aristodemus following him, and coming to the Lyceum he washed himself, as he would have done anywhere else, and after having spent the day there in his accustomed manner, went home in the evening.

Printed at The Riverside Press
for Houghton Mifflin Company
Boston and New York. Mcmviii.

440 copies. No. 203.

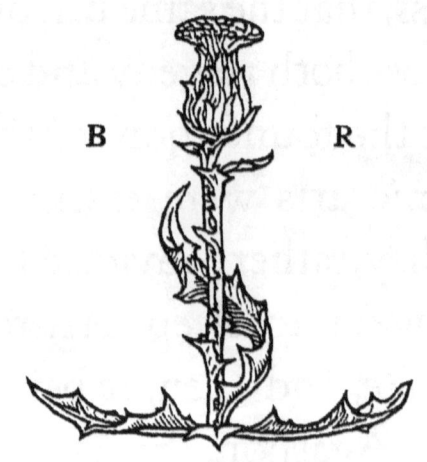

www.ingramcontent.com/pod-product-compliance
Lightning Source LLC
Chambersburg PA
CBHW020333170426
43200CB00006B/368